7707

31910

Rock Climbing

ROCK CLIMBING

Diana C. Gleasner
Photographs
by Bill Gleasner

David McKay Company, Inc.
New York

Library of Congress Cataloging in Publication Data

Gleasner, Diana C.
    Rock climbing.
    Includes index.
SUMMARY: Provides techniques of climbing and
information on equipment, safety, and places to climb.
    1. Rock climbing—Juvenile literature. [1. Rock
        climbing] I. Title.
    GV200.2.G57   796.5'223   80-7962
        ISBN 0-679-20925-5

1 2 3 4 5 6 7 8 9 10

MANUFACTURED IN THE UNITED STATES OF AMERICA

31910

For Bill

CONTENTS

Rock Climbing

1

Why Climb?

You stand at the base of a cliff and look up. It's obvious this straight up-and-down rock face was not meant to be climbed. You can't see any places to put hands or feet. Also, by hiking around one side and scrambling up from behind, you can reach the top without too much trouble. Then why are all these people standing around in hard hats, waiting to grapple with this wall of rock?

If you ask them what they're doing, they'll probably be glad to tell you. They may say that they intend to climb to the top of the cliff or that they're there to solve a rock problem. Ask them *why* they're going to all this trouble and you might be told that it's a great day for climbing. Or that this particular piece of stone is begging to be scaled. Some might just grin and tell you it's fun.

Stick around. You may find out what they mean by fun. If these are experts, you'll be amazed at how gracefully they almost flow up the cliff. Their fingers cling to tiny identations in the rock, notches so small that you can't see them. As the climbers move upward, these same invisible ridges support a toe or the edge of a shoe. Although they climb with a rope attached, they don't even touch it.

When one climber has reached the top, another may go up the same route in an entirely different manner. After you watch a few more, it becomes obvious there is no one "right" set of moves, but it's also clear that some climbers are more highly skilled than others. They ascend smoothly, with a rhythm of motion that makes it look almost easy. You, too, may want to try it.

If you're watching a class of beginners, the climbs won't look easy. You'll see them groping for a hold, straining to hang onto the rock, and grunting as they move. Some may even fall a few feet before the rope tightens and holds them dangling before the wall. As they attempt to climb, they may plaster themselves flat against the rock with arms outstretched above and legs trembling. You may wonder how they will ever be able to make progress with these uncooperative "sewing machine legs," as shaking limbs are known in the sport. You can be sure the climber is having a few doubts of his or her own.

Can this be fun?

Many moments in rock climbing are definitely not fun. But for those who enjoy learning new skills and meeting challenges, for those with a keen sense of adventure, rock climbing is a richly rewarding activity. And yes, it *is* fun.

Not everyone would define happiness as walking backward off a 150-foot cliff and sliding down a rope. Yet, climbers think rappelling is a marvelously efficient way to get to the bottom of things. Once they've summoned up the courage to take those first few steps, they say it's exhilarating.

Climbers, like scuba divers and kayakers, are a special

Happiness is finding the next handhold!

breed. They are individuals who are rarely tempted to follow the crowd blindly. Yet they are excellent team members who must be trusted to use common sense and good judgment. Otherwise, someone could be seriously injured or killed.

No one is more keenly aware of the dangers of the sport than experienced climbers. They know life in the outdoors is never totally predictable. Who can guarantee that a day which starts out sunny and clear won't end in a thunderstorm? Or that the tiny outcropping of rock you're about to put all your weight on won't break off? If it does, climbers may have more adventure than they care to handle.

The way to cut risks to a minimum is by starting with competent instruction. Because climbing has become a very popular activity, courses are readily available. Without an experienced climber to "show you the ropes," you are looking for disaster. To enjoy the enormous rewards of climbing, you will have to stay alive.

Is this sport for you? Yes, if you're not lazy and would like to solve problems, escape from the routine, and experience the freedom of high places. No, if you'd rather sit home and watch television. Certainly not, if you have a poor sense of balance.

You don't need to be a powerhouse of strength to participate, but you should be reasonably fit. Girls enjoy climbing as much as boys, and men and women of all ages are enthusiasts. Essential to success is your desire to learn. If you are really interested you will develop the agility and stamina needed on longer climbs.

You may be amazed to discover how important it is to use your brain. Just as surely as a muscle is strengthened by weightlifting, your mental agility will sharpen as you gain experience on the rocks. You must be able to concentrate totally on the problem ahead, to plan your moves, and to check and double-check your safety systems. In time, you'll gain the courage and self-confidence great climbers have in abundance.

Like most worthwhile things in life, rock climbing is not easy. As you stretch your limits to overcome problems on a mountain, you'll feel your mind and body fusing to meet the challenge. After you have mastered a difficult climb, you'll gain a new perspective. How satisfying to know you're capable of far more than you might have thought when you started.

Rock climbing was once considered just a part of mountaineering, one of many techniques needed to reach the summit. But it wasn't long before those who developed these specialized skills found they enjoyed the activity for itself. Climbing provided an intense, concentrated dose of living. They felt a new awareness of the beauty around them and a new respect for themselves. Now, of course, rock climbing has become an activity in its own right.

But what about getting to the top of the mountain? Isn't that really the point? Some say it is, but it's less important than you might think. Once you begin climbing, you'll understand this more clearly.

Beverly Johnson, a 120-pound women who is one of the best female rock climbers in the world, explained that while some of her friends rely heavily on strength and equipment, she depends more on balance and technique. She must have been doing something right to have been the first woman to solo climb the 3,000-foot vertical face of El Capitan in Yosemite Valley. She said, "To reach the summit was not my goal. My goal was the climb itself."

Well-known climber Pat Ament defines success in rock climbing as having control and exhibiting good judgment. According to him, "A day on the rock, whether I complete a route or 'fail,' may be perfectly successful as long as it is a controlled experience."

To many, rock climbing is more a philosophy than a sport; it's a way of life. One young man summed it up this way: "You come up here and face the mountain and on a given day you know you can take the hardest route and whip it. The next day you know you don't have it, and you don't even try. It's not competing with another person or group; it's not even a matter of trying to defeat the mountain. It's the knowledge that you have faced yourself and learned to live with what you find—or you keep trying until you can build a self you *do* respect."

This triumph of the human spirit is a rock climber's idea of what it means to win. Welcome to a sport where everyone can be a winner.

2

First Climbers

The ancient Greeks believed that the gods who controlled their lives lived on Mount Olympus, but no one dared climb up to see if the gods were attending to business. For hundreds and hundreds of years, mountains were off-limits to human beings. They were considered mysterious places where dragons, demons, and evil spirits lived. Besides, staying alive on level ground was enough of a challenge!

Mountains made interesting scenery, but to pry into their secrets was to ask for trouble. Their slopes sent "keep off" warnings in the form of landslides and floods. Yet, in the early 1700s, a few men began risking their lives in the Alps while searching for crystals or hunting ante-lopes.

About two hundred years ago, people's thoughts began to change. Scientists were solving some of the mysteries of the universe. If humans wanted to know more about their world, they would have to explore its heights.

7

Horace Bénédict de Saussure started learning about the highlands while collecting Alpine plants. He wondered if anyone would ever see the world from the top of France's Mont Blanc. At first the idea seemed as unreasonable as a trip to the moon. Blanc, at 15,782 feet, is the highest Alpine peak. But later, as his expeditions took him higher and higher into the mountains, Saussure thought it might be possible to scale Mont Blanc. In 1760, he offered a reward to the first man who reached the summit. Many tried. Some were killed in their attempts. Others went part way, then gave up. Finally, in 1786, Dr. Michel Paccard and his guide, Jacques Balmat, staggered to the top of Mont Blanc, their hearts pounding from altitude sickness, their fingers frostbitten.

The achievement did not go unnoticed. People in the little town at the base of the mountain had watched the two tiny specks of humanity struggle to the top. When they saw them standing on the summit, the townspeople began to cheer. The church bells of Chamonix rang wildly.

In other parts of the world, men began answering the challenge of the mountains. Their methods were often crude, but their spirit was indomitable. In 1827 two Norwegian farmers successfully scaled Romsdalshorn. Why? Because their friends had dared them to. How? By pushing and pulling each other up the peak.

Climbing became popular for the sheer joy of the activity, worth pursuing for itself rather than just to advance scientific knowledge. The Alps were the center of this climbing fever. There were more ascents between 1845 and 1865 than there had been in all the previous centuries combined.

Perhaps the best-known climb in modern times was the 1953 conquest of Mount Everest in the Himalayas of Nepal and Tibet. Everest, the world's highest peak, soars into the clouds 5½ miles above sea level. Its thin air, extremely steep walls, avalanches, crevasses, and strong winds have claimed many an expert mountaineer. After more than two months of tough climbing, Sir Edmund Hillary of New Zealand and Tenzing Norgay, a Nepalese tribesman, became the first to climb this mighty mountain. Queen Elizabeth II knighted Hillary for his magnificent achievement.

As mountain after mountain was successfully mastered, climbers looked for greater challenges. They tried more difficult routes up peaks that had been scaled from a different approach. Some increased the difficulties by braving ice and storms during the winter season, while others went solo.

Today more than a half-million people climb with some regularity. Many find enough challenges to stretch their mental and physical resources within a few miles of their homes. Others dream of far-off peaks, as yet unconquered, in China, New Guinea, or Antarctica. All share the proud heritage of early climbers who opened the way to great adventure.

3

Rock Climbing, U.S.A.

The lure of climbing has always meant challenge and adventure. Early pioneers in this country had more challenges than they really needed. Their courage and resourcefulness were tested at every turn, and life in the wilderness was a daily adventure. They might climb a tree to look for Indians or a hill for a better view to plot their course across the prairies. But to climb for sport would have been considered an outrageous waste of time. As for mountains, they were obstacles standing in the way of westward travel. The idea was to find the least difficult way around or through them.

Curiosity is a potent force. Sooner or later the drive to know what's there sends people into the depths of the ocean or the farthest reaches of space. In 1806, Zebulon Pike was leading a party exploring the wilderness in what is now Colorado when he saw in the distance a mountain that looked like a blue cloud. He felt he had to discover the peak, to know what it was like at the summit.

The men headed for the mountain, but greatly under-estimated the distance to its base. Not only were supplies low when they started climbing, but their summer clothing proved poor protection against the cold and snow awaiting them at higher altitudes. The crowning disillusionment came when they reached the "top" and found that the real peak still lay ahead. It wasn't until 1820 that Pikes Peak was finally conquered. Although the rough conditions made the feat a real accomplishment, rock climbing skills, as we know them, were not necessary. Fitness and determination were enough to propel those first American mountaineers to the summit.

The traditional reason for climbing a mountain—"because it is there"—eventually led men up the snowy sides of Mount Rainier in the Pacific Northwest. This impressive peak could be seen on any clear day from the newly settled communities of Tacoma and Seattle. A full fifty years after the climbing of Pikes Peak, it captured the imagination of a local newspaper editor who became the first white man to reach the top.

These isolated climbing successes soon gave way to the business of settling a new country. In the 1860s, government surveyors scaled mountains in order to map the surrounding land. Lugging heavy equipment and supplies, these men struggled to the tops of many of the great western peaks, including California's Mount Whitney. By 1900, most of the highest mountains in the United States had been scaled.

Climbing became a popular day's outing. Local guides forged the easiest way to the top and charged a fee to take large parties up the slopes. Men and women, eager for a novel experience and a great view, clambered up Mount Rainier, Mount Whitney, and Longs Peak in Colorado.

Social rock scrambling was one thing, serious climbing quite another. Outdoor enthusiasts and climbers on the East Coast formed the Appalachian Mountain Club of Boston. When they got wind of the stirring achievements of the prestigious Alpine Club of London, they began to think in terms of tackling great snow-clad peaks.

Not to be outdone by their British counterparts, Americans formed their own Alpine Club in 1902. The Alps, complete with glaciers and avalanches, represented the ultimate experience of the day. A few brave souls headed for the closest thing they could find on this continent, the Canadian Rockies, and conquered some of the most challenging peaks. Fired by competitive zeal, club members were soon making an impressive number of first ascents abroad as well as in North America.

Climbers of this period were, at best, poorly equipped. Nailed boots were standard, and everyone carried a huge ice ax. Lightweight gear was unknown. Joined by a taut rope, climbing parties bet their lives on the time-honored notion that the leader never falls. More than a few groups fell to oblivion when someone slipped and yanked the others off a mountain.

Great peaks tested climbers' courage and challenged their resourcefulness. Techniques included whatever was necessary to make upward progress including standing on each other's shoulders. Because their rock climbing skills and their safety measures were so inadequate, most climbers opted for the quickest way to the top.

Few people bothered with local cliffs. They didn't fit the Alpine image that was considered to be "real" climbing. One exception was Albert Ellingwood, a professor at Colorado College. He began to tackle rock problems in his own backyard, the Flatirons of the Rocky Mountains. While other Coloradoans were intent on hiking up as many peaks as they could, Ellingwood sought out more and more difficult climbs. Because the potential for disaster was ever present, he worked out a primitive belay system for protection. As he was able to master more and more difficult routes, his confidence grew. Finally, Elling-wood tackled the 350-foot volcanic plug on the top of Lizard Head, a feat generally regarded as impossible. A few strategically placed spikes overcame the lack of hand-holds and footholds on the sheer sides. He had some close calls, but they only made his final victory seem particularly sweet. Having climbed the "unclimbable," a jubilant Ellingwood rappelled down the steep face of the spire. A new era in climbing was under way.

During the 1930s, the University of Colorado held a series of rock climbing classes. Spectacular red rock formations in the Garden of the Gods attracted enthusi-asts who scaled them for sport as well as to condition themselves for larger expeditions. There were enough climbers around to warrant the publication of a guidebook to the Flatirons. Perhaps most important, imaginations were fired by an exchange of ideas at a joint meeting of the Appalachian Mountain Club and the Colorado Moun-tain Club.

Easterners had begun to discover the excitement to be found on local cliffs. At first they thought of them as strictly a training ground for a "real" climb, which to them meant a European experience. They scaled quarry walls with candle lanterns in their teeth to ready them-selves for 3 A.M. starts in the Alps.

Major advances in techniques began to take place on the Shawangunks, about a hundred miles north of New York City. These 200-foot cliffs presented a variety of technical problems. Cracks and chimneys were a rarity. Climbers had to overcome sheer vertical faces and difficult overhangs. They began to use pitons for aid in making progress upward, as well as for protection.

Few Californians at the time were thinking in terms of traditional mountain climbing. Many were local boys, looking for adventure within easy reach of home. While Alpine Club members were grappling with the tough

13

Rock climbing.

problems presented by Alaska's Mount McKinley in terms of access, weather, and endurance, these climbers concentrated on sheer rock walls. As their skill level advanced, they found themselves in increasingly treacherous situations. Practicing safety belays became an integral part of their rock work. They experimented with equipment, using 10-inch nails for pitons and learning to place an expansion bolt. A few even ordered expensive carabiners from Germany (see Glossary of Climbing Terms).

World War II brought recreational climbing to a halt. But the technology that resulted from the war effort brought significant advances both in quality and availability of equipment. Nylon rope proved far superior to the old natural fiber standbys. Pitons and carabiners became available at a reasonable cost. New lightweight survival gear was easier to carry and made camping out infinitely more endurable.

A new type of climber appeared on the scene, no longer strictly from the upper classes, with unlimited money and leisure to travel around the world. Working-class men and women, looking for a weekend outing, joined the white-collar professionals in search of exercise and adventure. This diverse group of enthusiasts substituted energy, ambition, and competition for the hallowed traditions of Alpine climbing. Progress was swift.

The era eliminated one climb after another from the "impossible" category. Presiding grandly over the wilderness scene in Yosemite Valley was the 3,000-foot monolith, El Capitan. In the early 1950s no one even considered climbing it. El Cap was overwhelming in size; it seemed to take up the whole sky. Besides, there were no places to rest on its smooth flank. Psychologically, a climb was inconceivable.

Inevitably, a talented band of rock experts one day squinted up at the great wall, seeing it for the first time as something other than scenery. First came the dream, then the decision to try El Capitan. Practical problems were as complex as the rock was huge. Climbers coped with its incredible size by establishing a series of camps, which they linked to the ground by fixed ropes. They could restock their supplies in this way. Progress was agonizingly slow. After a week of arduous effort, their ropes reached 1,000 feet up the wall.

These climbers faced none of the traditional Alpine challenges—difficult access, bitter cold, and isolation. But there were other problems. They consumed great quantities of water because of the enormous effort expended under a torrid sun. Liquids were heavy and difficult to haul up, so they learned to limit themselves to smaller quantities. The overcrowded park was full of tourists who tied up traffic as they gawked at the climbers inching their way up the massive walls. Finally, officials banned climbing until after Labor Day. A series of complications prohibited the group from returning until one year later. After spending a total of forty-five days on the wall, they won the summit after an all-out, eleven-day push. The conquest of El Capitan in 1958 was a major landmark in American rock climbing.

Before the 1960s climbers were isolated. Groups in the Tetons had no idea what was going on in New York. Yosemite regulars were unaware of progress being made on Colorado cliffs. When the word began to get around, so did the climbers. They wanted to know if they were as skilled as they thought they were. Rumors of impossible climbs and improbable achievements were enough to send a group across the country. More often than not their goal was to steal a first ascent from the locals.

All serious rock climbers eventually wound up in California's Yosemite Valley. Tales of multi-day climbs on mammoth granite walls were too much to resist. During the 1960s the national park was the scene of the most intense rock climbing in the country. A semipermanent climbing community sprang up. For the first time, men and women made climbing the focus of their lives. They quit school, took odd jobs in the off season, and set about to prove themselves on the rock. Dreams of forging first ascents on great walls consumed them. There was no point in bothering to plan for tomorrow. The valley had enough challenges to last a lifetime.

By this time women were beginning to take the lead on some of the country's most challenging climbs. They had come a long way. In the early 1900s climbing clubs had prohibited them from being seen in their knickers until they were well away from camp. An occasional woman braved the censure of society and climbed with her husband, but most stayed home where they were told they belonged.

The women's movement and the ecology trends of the time brought women to the cliffs. Two of the most talented made the first all-female ascent of El Capitan. A woman's team scaled Mount McKinley. In 1965 another pair climbed the forbidding north face of the Grand Teton. The climb was widely acknowledged to be the most arduous, all-woman ascent ever made on this continent.

Beverly Johnson built her reputation on the big walls of Yosemite. Of her monumental achievement on El Capitan, she said, "You climb a big wall the same way you eat an elephant, one bite at a time." Although she was the first woman to solo climb El Cap, she said it was not her most difficult ascent. The Leaning Tower, a 1,200-foot overhanging wall in Yosemite Valley holds that distinction. Her attitude is philosophical. "Once you are committed to the climb," she said, "there's no turning back. Death is a part of mountaineering. You know what the risks are, that it can happen, and you accept that."

By the 1970s the big walls were no longer the formidable psychological barriers they had once been. First ascents were harder to come by. The emphasis shifted from what you climbed to how you climbed it. Routes that had originally been tackled with direct aid were now done free. Clean climbing became the new standard.

The greatest change in the 1980s has been the tremendous new wave of interest and participants. Climbing classes, schools, and clubs appear at the base of every cliff. Everyone seems to have a carabiner. Rope handling and safety measures are widely taught, with the result that climbing is safer than ever. Techniques and skills are advancing at an awesome rate.

The history of rock climbing is the story of people solving problems that seemed insoluble, scaling for speed the routes that would never "go," and handling impossible rocks in elegant style.

Today's climbers are finding adventure above every handhold. Over the next ridge they may take on the current "impossible" climb. The sky is getting closer all the time.

4

Equipment

Climbing is not a costly sport, especially in the beginning. Your major expense will be for instruction, if you're not lucky enough to have an experienced friend to teach you. Dress comfortably in clothes meant for rugged use. Jeans that are too tight will keep you from moving freely on the rock, and loose ends like shirttails and scarves should be avoided. They might become entangled in the rope on a rappel and create a very dangerous situation. A waterproof parka is a good idea, because temperatures have a way of dropping unexpectedly in the mountains.

Tennis shoes or hiking boots work well for most climbing until you get into advanced rock work. Whether you choose a flexible or a stiff shoe will depend a great deal on what kind of climbing you'll be doing and where. Certain areas lend themselves to a stiffer shoe, but don't buy anything special for climbing until you find out what the climbers you're with prefer.

Flexible shoes provide a better grip on rough sloping

Basic climbing equipment consists of a safety helmet, quality climbing rope, carabiner, and nylon webbing for making a Swiss seat.

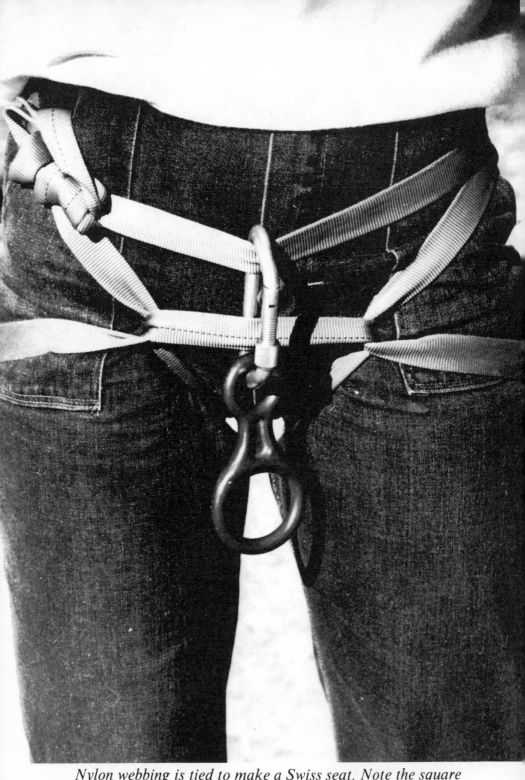

Nylon webbing is tied to make a Swiss seat. Note the square knot and overhand safety knots.

rocks, fit into narrow openings, and allow you to feel the rock better. Stiff shoes are preferred for standing on small edges; they can be wedged into cracks more easily and are more comfortable for hiking. They're also less slippery on wet rocks or pine needle-covered slopes. Because shoes get scuffed up, you might want to make yours last longer by coating the stitching with epoxy glue.

You may hear someone mention special rock climbing shoes, called Klettershoes. These are lightweight and have rubber part way up the sides and on the toe and heel. The rubber helps the foot adhere to the rock and protects the shoe from abrasion. However, Klettershoes have become quite expensive, and they aren't at all necessary for the beginning climber.

A hard hat designed especially for climbing may be purchased in a sporting goods or mountaineering store, but yours will probably be provided if you've signed up for instruction. The value of a helmet cannot be overemphasized, as rocks and equipment falling from above are major causes of injury. Even a tiny object that has fallen a long way can be fatal if your head is unprotected.

The single most important item of equipment is the rope—a climber's lifeline. Until you get into advanced aid climbing, the rope is used to protect you in case of a fall. You never pull yourself up with it unless there's an emergency. But if you should slip, the rope is your only link to your partners, and it must be absolutely reliable. Standard climbing ropes are 150 feet long and 7/16 of an inch in diameter. Most have a breaking strength of more than 5,000 pounds. A rope is the most expensive piece of equipment used in the sport, but yours will probably be provided by the school or club teaching you to climb. Some inexperienced youngsters have headed for the mountains with a clothesline, but not all of them were lucky enough to return.

Even if you don't have to purchase a climbing rope,

you should know something about the different types and how to care for them. The best quality ropes for rock work are nylon. Most of them are made in Europe and are called Perlon, the European name for nylon. Synthetic fibers are superior in many ways to natural fibers like manila, sisal, and cotton. Their ability to stretch means the rope can absorb the shock of a fall far better than a natural fiber rope. In addition to this vital elasticity, synthetic ropes do not mildew; they are stronger, more durable, and easier on your hands.

Nylon climbing ropes are made of either twisted or kernmantel construction. Because a twisted rope (sometimes called hard-lay, mountain-lay, or laid rope) consists of three or four strands entwined around each other, it can be easily inspected by separating the strands. Despite this advantage, most climbers prefer kernmantel construction, which is more expensive but has some features that compensate for the added cost. The smooth surface is easier to handle, and it slides with less friction over the rock and through various pieces of climbing hardware. This happens because the nylon filaments are braided to form a core (kern) and are covered by a smooth, woven sheath (mantel). Kernmantel rope doesn't kink as much as twisted rope, and it is impervious to water. But its distinct drawback is that you can't examine the core fibers for damage. Because of this, a rope should be replaced after it has held a long fall. A climbing rope has a fairly short life span, but better the rope have this problem than the climber.

Knowing the history of a climbing rope is essential. For this reason, you should never buy a used rope or lend yours to anyone other than a trustworthy and competent fellow climber. Inspect the rope by running it slowly through your hands before every climb and each time it is stepped on or hit by a rock. Be especially careful if someone else has used the rope previously. If you have

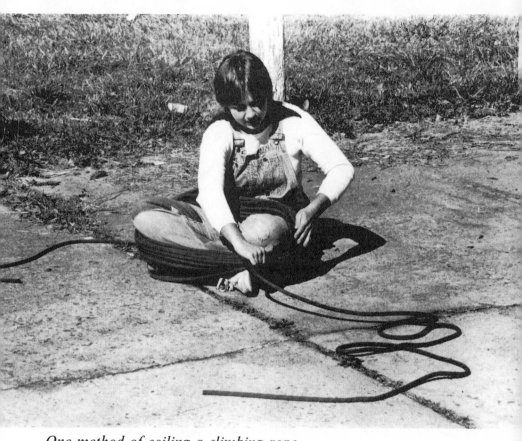

One method of coiling a climbing rope.

The correct way to carry a coiled rope.

doubts about it, throw it out, but before you do, cut it in small sections so someone else doesn't trust his or her well-being to it.

You can prolong the life of a rope by taking good care of it. If it is wet, uncoil it and dry it thoroughly before recoiling. The rope should be stored in a cool, dry place, loosely coiled. It should never be stepped on or dragged in the dirt. Tiny particles of sand may work their way inside the fibers and cut them. Don't leave it outdoors unnecessarily because sunlight weakens the filaments. Never store a rope in a car trunk or near grease, paints, acids, or solvents. If the rope has been in a coil for a long time, it may have a few kinks. These can be removed by letting it unwind from a high place or by dragging it full length over a clean, smooth surface. You may have to repeat the process several times if the rope has been wet or is new.

Webbing is an essential item of climbing equipment. One-inch nylon webbing can be arranged around the legs and pelvic area in a diaperlike harness, known as a "Swiss seat," or tied around the waist to make a "swami" belt. Don't forget that webbing wears more quickly than rope and that leaving it out in the sun will seriously weaken it.

You'll need a carabiner to clip into the climbing rope or to tie into a fixed anchor. Carabiners are available in both aluminum and steel, but aluminum is preferred because it is lighter in weight and provides ample strength. Purchase your carabiner in a reputable mountaineering store, and be sure it tests to hold at least 2,500 pounds. The modified D-shape is more expensive than the oval, but considerably stronger. Your life depends on this piece of equipment, so beware of older models that are second-hand.

5

Knots

Some day you may be halfway down a 150-foot rappel and happen to glance at your Swiss seat. The square knot that holds the seat together is all that is keeping you from crashing to the rocks below. Or you may be clambering up a sheer face when a foothold suddenly crumbles and you fall a few feet before you are stopped by the rope held by your belayer. Luckily, the belayer is anchored to the mountain by a snug bowline knot. Only in one of these life-or-death situations will you truly appreciate the importance of knot tying.

All serious climbers know their lives depend on the knots they tie. They can buy the strongest, most expensive climbing rope available, but if they can't tie a knot correctly, they might as well trust their lives to clothesline. Knot-tying is not difficult. Climbers don't need to know dozens and dozens of variations, but they must be able to tie a few knots well under the most trying circumstances.

One instructor tells his students that they may some-

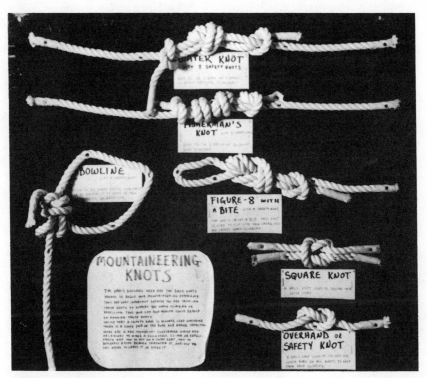

Basic rock climbing knots.

day have to tie their knots while someone else is screaming at them or when they are cold and wet or while they are hanging upside down. He also points out that all these things might well be happening at the same time. This is why instructors advise students to practice tying their knots in the dark, behind their backs, and in a cold shower. Someday, this ability may save their lives.

Learn to use a few basic knots well. You'll be surprised how versatile they will be. Climbing knots must be very strong and relatively easy to tie. They must retain their shape under intense strain. Also, they must not be too difficult to untie.

Inspect knots frequently because they have a way of untying themselves, particularly in nylon rope or webbing. Check the knots in your Swiss seat after each rappel and certainly after every fall. Most knots can be protected against accidental loosening by securing each loose end with an overhand knot.

6

Learning to Climb

The best way to learn to climb is to scramble around on some rocks with an experienced friend. Slab climbing, the term for trying out low-angle slopes, can be great fun. It also gives you a chance to practice the basic techniques you will need as you progress to more demanding situations.

The position of your body is all important. Stand as upright as possible, holding yourself away from the rock. You may want to follow your natural instincts, but they can quickly lead to bad habits. Beginners tend to lean into the rock as the angle of the climb becomes steeper, rather than keeping their weight over their feet. When you cling to the rock, you can't see as well, you're shifting too much weight to your arms, and there is a much greater tendency for your feet to slip.

Good balance enables you to do most of the work with your legs. Because they have the largest muscles and are so much stronger than the arms, it makes sense to

31

Scrambling on low angle rocks (slab climbing) is a good way to learn the basics.

depend on them as much as possible. Remember that good climbers never use their knees. It's considered very poor form. Besides, it's hard on the joints.

You should tackle a cliff the way you climb the rungs of a ladder, with your weight going straight down into your shoes and your hands guiding you. Many beginners find standing straight very difficult. After a while, you'll realize that you get better traction when your body is away from the rock, even if you may really want to hug it. On steep cliffs, where your hands and arms get a strenuous workout, the habit of good balance will help you conserve energy.

Keep your arms as low as possible. By choosing holds that are fairly close together, you lessen the strain on them and you don't have as great a tendency to throw yourself out of balance. Try not to let your arms and legs stretch out full length at the same time. If you do, you'll get that where-do-I-go-from-here feeling. Keep three limbs in contact with the cliff (two feet and a hand or two hands and a foot), and use the fourth to move upward.

Learn to plan ahead, using your eyes to select a sequence of moves. Then ascend as smoothly as possible. Think in terms of flowing upward calmly and deliberately. Even on easy climbs, pick every step with care and move as gracefully as possible. Rest, whenever you can, in a position where your muscles are not straining.

Knowledgeable climbers never trust their weight to plants. Small trees or bushes that grow in the mountains rarely have a root system deep enough to hold a person. Be careful not to climb directly above another climber; rocks that you loosen can cause serious injury.

It's a good idea for beginners to climb with a rope, even when the slope is fairly gentle. When you get into face climbing, a rope is a necessity. Whenever a rope or other piece of equipment is used for protection, the sport is referred to as technical climbing.

Be sure the rope is properly secured to a climber before ascent. Note the bowline knot.

As you graduate from scrambling on slabs to climbing a steep rock face, you'll need to use a variety of holds to make your ascent. As the angle increases, these rock protrusions become more important. Test each hold by tugging, thumping, or kicking before trusting your weight to it. A hollow sound or a slight movement is a warning that even the most solid-looking rock may be surprisingly fragile.

The most basic handhold is referred to as a cling hold. The best ones have a good edge for gripping, and are called buckets or jug handles. Some are straight, square-cut ledges that may be only wide enough to serve as a fingerhold.

Handholds quickly become footholds as you make progress upward. Square ledges, large enough for your whole foot, are fine if you can find them. But most of the time, you'll be getting no more than a toehold or the tip of a toehold. The outside edge of the big toe often works best. Try to keep the heel below the level of your toes. Once you've settled on your foot position, don't change it. Moving your heel upward is an invitation to trouble.

Another way to use your feet to advantage, especially if you are wearing flexible shoes, is frictioning or smearing. Cover the hold with the sole, then twist it so the lower side of the foot next to the rock is worked into the depression. Push downward and inward on the hold. This works on the theory that the more rubber you have touching the rock, the better your foot can grip it.

Manteling is a useful technique on a smooth ledge that slopes downward and outward. This type of ledge may be useless as a cling hold, but may work very well as a pressure hold. Place the heels of your hands on the sloping surface, with your elbows pointed upward, and press yourself up onto the ledge. The motion resembles the one used to boost yourself up onto the edge of a swimming pool, except that instead of kicking to get

Two rock faces coming together at right angles (open book) create a climbing challenge.

Stand up straight, with your body away from the rock in a ladder-climbing position.

momentum, you depend on legwork on the rock. Even the narrowest edge can be used as a brief toehold to take enough weight off the arms to make the move possible. This takes more strength than your everyday cling holds, and you have to be flexible enough to hoist your foot up on the mantel.

Manteling on ledges above your head may take considerable practice. Sometimes you can do a one-handed mantel; other times you'll have to use one hand on top of the other. Occasionally there will be enough room for both hands on the mantel. If you can, space your hands about a foot apart with the fingers pointing toward each other. Remember that when you swing your legs up onto the ledge, you're less likely to slip if you keep your hips up and away from the rock. Your feet will get better friction this way.

A variation of the position for manteling is used to move sideways on a ledge. The secret of a successful hand traverse is to use your feet rather than let your legs dangle. Even if the feet are working against a sheer wall, they can help. Because your arms are holding up so much of your body weight, the maneuver is a strenuous one. It's best done fairly quickly, before you run out of arm power.

Jamming is a technique for places in which narrow cracks must be used in place of well-defined holds. Clinging to a handhold is a natural move; jamming is not, and must be learned. The idea is to wedge a part of the body into a crack in order to hold the climber in place so he can move upward. Finger, hand, and fist jams are easily mastered and, with practice, can be done without even scratching the skin. If the crack is too narrow for your hand, you can sometimes slide your fingers in and curl them enough so they won't easily slip out. Usually it works better with the thumb pointed downward, especially if you need to twist the fingers for a better grip.

Relax your hand as you insert it in the crack to find

A useful technique for getting over a ledge is a pressure hold, called mantling.

Keep your arms low and look for holds that are fairly close together.

the most solid position for an open hand jam. With fingers together or apart and the hand bent at the palm, tighten it to lock in place. One of the secrets of success in jamming is to use only as much strength as is necessary to accomplish each move. Overgripping or any kind of unnecessary straining will tire you quickly.

To make a fist jam, ease your hand into a crack with the palm toward the back of the opening, and make a fist. When you turn the fist, the hand will expand and grip the sides. This hold can't support a great deal of weight, but you'll be surprised at how effective it can be for a quick move.

An elbow jam might work in a crack too large for a hand jam. To tighten the elbow, make it bulge by pulling your fist back toward the shoulder. Although this is not a terribly strong hold, it may be just the ticket out of a tight spot.

Foot jamming is easy enough. Simply wedge your shoe into a crack by inserting it on an angle. Then straighten your knee so you can put your weight on it.

A crack wide enough for the whole body is called a chimney. Most chimney climbing is readily learned. You can usually jam yourself into the opening by bracing your back against one side and pushing against the other side with your feet. By exerting pressure in opposite directions, you can make progress upward.

There are a number of different ways to climb a chimney. You can work your legs up while your arms support your body, and then move your arms while your legs hold you in place. Or you can place one leg back under your hips and push upward with it, then repeat the process with the other foot under the hips. To rest, simply lock your legs in an extended position.

If the crack narrows, you might find a toe-and-heel foot jam effective. The toe is pressed against the far wall and the heel against the back wall. Eventually, the chimney may become too small for anything but wriggling upward by applying pressure on both walls with any part of the body available.

Wider chimneys call for bridging. Straddle the opening with one foot and hand on one side and the other foot and hand on the opposite wall. Remember to keep three points of contact with the rock and to move one limb at a time. This technique can also be used to scale right-angle corners with holds on both sides. You'll find you are better able to make use of any available holds even though you may feel more exposed.

One of the most strenuous types of holds is the lieback. It takes a lot of effort because it relies on opposing forces to make progress. This means one muscle must strain against the other. The hands, which use the crack as a cling hold, pull while the feet push against the wall for friction. Hands and feet move alternately upward, a little bit at a time. Keep your arms extended so that the bones, rather than the muscles, do most of the work. Feet should be kept high enough so that they don't slip. However, if they're too high, the arms will tire quickly. The trick is not to strain any more than necessary while moving deliberately and rapidly.

Downclimbing

The ability to climb back down a rock wall is as important as being able to climb up. Sometimes it may be even more so. Expert climbers keep downclimbing in mind when they ascend a rock. It's part of their habit of thinking ahead. They have no intention of getting themselves into a spot from which they cannot move up or down. Good climbing is controlled movement, and part of the control comes from knowing you can reverse a route. Sometimes this skill may be vital in order to find

Keeping three points of contact on the rock, move one limb at a time.

a better path up the mountain. Because the success of the climb may depend on it, it's a good idea to practice downclimbing to get used to the feeling.

Downclimbing doesn't feel as natural as climbing up. Part of the awkwardness is because it's difficult to see. Your body blocks your view of what is below you. Face outward as long as you can, and when the wall becomes too steep, turn sideways to pick out your footholds. On a vertical wall you're going to have to face the cliff as you descend. Lean out occasionally to look below and use your feet to feel for holds. As in ascending, you'll want to keep three points of contact with the cliff, while planning your moves in small sequences whenever possible.

7

Belaying

Belaying is the most important skill a climber learns. The purpose of a belay is to stop a person who is falling. The word comes from a sailing term, which means securing something with a rope. When you belay someone, you serve as the anchor for him. You protect the climber by wrapping the rope part way around your body and reacting immediately when he or she begins to fall.

The split-second action a belayer takes is possible because he or she has practiced until the response is automatic. In a crisis, climbers won't have time to think which hand they should use to stop the fall. The skill is not difficult to learn, but it must be thoroughly mastered. The life of the climber is literally in the hands of the belayer.

Even the weakest member of a climbing team can safely serve as a belayer because the fall is stopped by friction rather than strength. The safest and best position is the sitting hip belay. You wrap the rope around your

The anchor rope should be tied snugly into the belayer's waist so that a fall will not pull him out of position.

hips, then take it in as the climber below you works his or her way up the rock. Your hands must be trained to react instinctively. The hand holding the rope going to the climber is the guiding hand. Some people call it the feeling hand. It is the hand that pulls in the rope to keep it from becoming slack as the climber ascends. The hand on the opposite side of your body, which holds the weight in case of a fall, is called the holding or braking hand. The braking hand never lets go of the rope. If the climber slips, the friction generated by the rope going around your body enables you to hold the other climber fast.

Before you assume the position for a belay, you must find a suitable location. This place is known as a belay ledge or a belay stance. The ideal spot would be a depression, with room to spread your legs and places to brace your feet. There should be a fixed point behind you where you can secure yourself to the cliff with at least two anchors. You could use a sturdy tree, a rock outcropping, or a piton. The anchor rope should be tied snugly to the belayer's waist so that a fall does not pull the belayer out of position.

The belayer should be in a direct line between the potential fall and the anchor. The body is braced toward the direction of the pull. Usually the belayer's back is toward the wall and the leg on the side of the pull is locked straight.

As the belayer, you hold the climber's lifeline in your hands, and should give the situation your complete attention. You must always be ready for an emergency. If you let go of the rope with your braking hand, even for a moment, you are not prepared for action. Each time the brake hand must move to take up slack, you use the guide hand to help hold the rope. If there is a fall, the braking hand immediately clamps down on the rope. You can create even more friction by throwing the braking hand in front of your waist. It takes practice to hold the weight

47

A belayer protecting the climber.

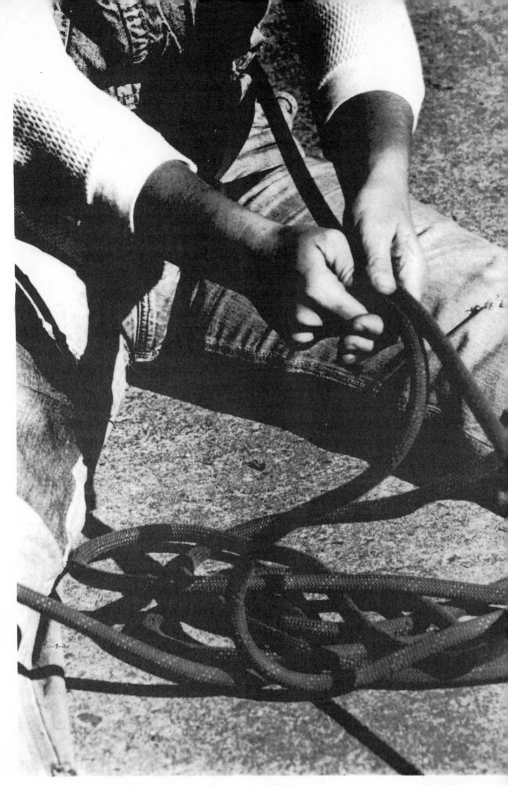

The braking hand never lets go of the rope.

A safe belay ledge provides a place to brace the feet.

with the braking hand, but it's extremely important. The guide hand cannot possibly hold a fall of any consequence.

Practice first on level ground. The climber should walk slowly toward the belayer and then suddenly run in the opposite direction. The run will give the belayer an idea of how a fall will feel. When belayers can react instantaneously, they are ready for a session on the rock. There, the two can practice belaying with all the climber's weight off the ground.

As a belayer pulls in the rope, the hands move in opposite directions. Each time the guiding hand is returned to its original position, it grips the rope in front of the braking hand, enabling the braking hand to slide back along the rope. Keep the line taut between you and the climber, but be careful not to overdo it and pull him or her off balance. Too much slack can create a potentially dangerous situation. A climber might fall too far before being stopped and hit a rock or ledge. Excessive slack might mean that a fall is so forceful it is out of the belayer's control. This could result in severe rope burns on the hands of the belayer and possible disaster for the climber.

The standing hip belay and the standing shoulder belay take less room than the sitting hip belay, but are not quite as stable. All the same principles and precautions apply. Every time you belay, the system should be checked and rechecked. Make sure the knots are secure on the anchor and that you lay the rope in a compact pile as you pull it in. On a belay stance, where there is scarcely enough room for your feet, the belayer stands leaning against the cliff. In this half-standing position, you can sit back on the rope in case of a fall.

It is essential that climbing signals be clear and that there is no chance for misunderstanding. Climbers have their own standardized calls and answers. If a call is not answered properly, find out why before proceeding. Never

51

The climber's safety depends on the belayer's total concentration.

The guiding hand grips both ropes so that the braking hand can move back along rope.

Standing hip belay. Note the tree used as an anchor.

assume a signal has been heard until you get an answer. Call out loud and clear, especially on blustery days and when your teammates are out of sight.

The climber asks, "Belay on?" to find out if the belayer is anchored and ready. When the belayer answers, "On belay," he is fully ready to protect the climber. The climber calls, "Climbing," to indicate he's ready to begin his ascent. The belayer answers, "Climb," which means that it's okay to go ahead. If the climber wants the belayer to take in more rope to get rid of the slack, he shouts, "Up rope!" If he needs more rope, he calls "Slack." Be careful not to confuse things by calling, "Take up the slack," when you mean "Up rope."

"Rock" is a warning to those below that something has been dislodged or dropped and may hit them. "Tension" means to pull in on the rope as hard as possible and hold it tight. When climbers lose their footing, they yell, "Prepare for fall!" or "Falling!" to warn the belayer that immediate action is necessary.

When climbers no longer need the protection of the belayer, they call, "Off belay." They should be absolutely safe before they give this signal, because serious accidents have occurred when climbers were too quick to dispense with the safety system. The belayer answers the climber's "Off belay" with "Belay off," confirming that he or she is no longer responsible for the climber. "Rope" is a call that alerts those below to watch out because a rope is being thrown.

8

Rappelling

Rappelling is a way for a climber to descend from a steep cliff by a controlled slide down a rope. The term *rappel* is derived from a French word meaning "to recall." Usually the rope is doubled so that it can be retrieved or recalled by pulling on one end. Whichever rappel method you use, the purpose is to provide enough friction so you can be lowered slowly and deliberately.

Rappelling in the movies often looks extremely exciting. Stunt men add drama to a scene by bouncing and springing down the mountain in long jolting leaps. This may be all right for show business, but it puts a tremendous strain on the equipment.

The most critical part of the rappel system is the anchor. It must be sound. Unlike the belay anchor, which provides a backup system of protection, the rappel anchor is often the only thing between you and the ground below. Most accidents are caused by its failure. A sturdy tree, rock knob, or even a couple of pitons—spaced to divide

58

The author is rappelling on a fire tower during a class practice session.

the strain—will serve well. Make sure that two or more loops or slings are independently tied to it. If one sling breaks, the second serves as a backup. Don't trust an anchor left by another group of climbers. Even if it looks new, a sling found at the site has probably been weakened by having ropes pulled through it. Also, sunlight damages nylon webbing in a short time.

As in all other aspects of climbing, a cautious attitude determines how safe a rappel will be. Extreme care should be taken with every detail. Rappelling is fairly simple and straightforward, but it requires complete concentration on the part of the climbers. Even though they are tired or rushing to get off the mountain because of an approaching storm, they must have the patience to check each part of the system.

When you can't see to the bottom of the rappel, you should yell, "Rope!" before tossing it out. Then wait for a moment so that any climbers below can get out of the way. Throw the rope away from the wall so that it doesn't get hung up. One way to keep it from tangling is to throw half of the coils out first and then immediately toss the second half.

The simplest method of rappelling uses only a rope, and is called a body rappel, or the Dulfersitz (Dulfer for short). Facing the anchor point, straddle the doubled rope and reach behind to grasp it. Bring it forward around the left hip, across the chest, over the right shoulder, and down across the back to be held in the left hand. Your palm should be forward with the thumb downward. The left hand is then used as the controlling, or braking, hand while the right holds the rope loosely and is used mainly for balance.

You can reverse the way the rope is wrapped around the body by starting it around the right hip. Remember the braking hand is on the same side as the wrapped hip. Also, it is always the lower hand that holds the free end

Figure eight clipped into a carabiner.

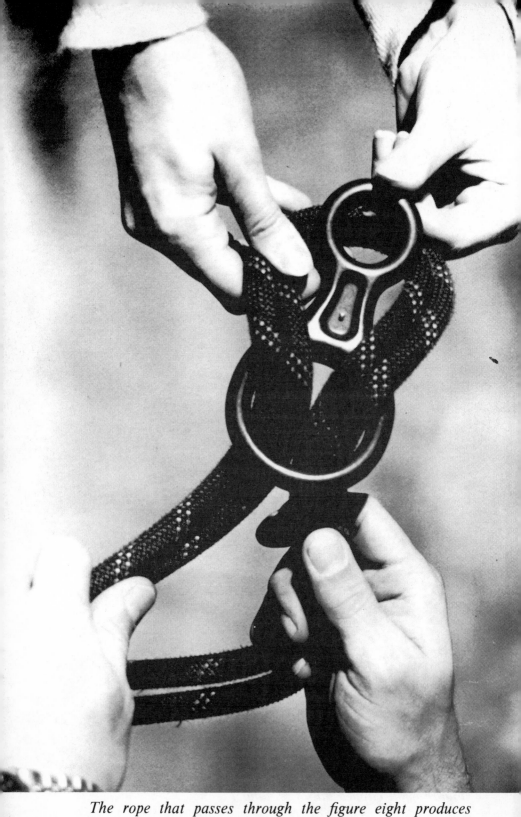

The rope that passes through the figure eight produces friction for a controlled descent.

This climber is correctly outfitted for the brake system of rappelling.

The lower hand (braking hand) controls the descent.

of the rope, which is heading downward. Never release the braking hand from the rope. If you need to let go for any reason, do so with the upper hand.

Now, in a semi-sitting position facing the cliff, walk slowly backward. The first step takes some courage, but once you're on your way, it's not at all difficult. You'll find it easy to brake with your lower hand. Your upper body should lean out enough so that your feet press in, with the soles flat against the rock. Your legs should be about a shoulder-width apart with the knees bent. Lower yourself slowly and smoothly, controlling your descent with the braking hand. If you go too fast, the friction of the rope going over the hip and shoulder may cause a rope burn. For more control, simply press the rope under and against the buttock with the brake hand. Some extra padding may be needed, particularly if the rappel is a long one, because the Dulfersitz creates more friction than any other type of rappel. Always keep the wrapped leg slightly lower than the other one so that it won't come unwrapped. Try not to place your legs too high—never above your body.

If you should end up on a ledge when you have finished your descent, anchor yourself before detaching the rope. Only after you are secured do you shout, "Off rappel!" There is a good reason for this added caution. When you are down, there is a natural tendency to relax and think you're out of danger. Too many climbers have descended safely to a narrow ledge, called, "Off rappel," and immediately fallen backward off the cliff. Sometimes they have been thrown off balance when they released the rope. Or, perhaps they forgot that good climbers never let their guard down until they are safely off the mountain.

The beauty of the Dulfersitz, or body rappel, is that it needs no extra equipment. It's useful on a gradual rock incline when a quick descent is needed. Because it has

Rappel practice from a fire tower. The climber descends the wall while the belayer (on a safety net) protects him from below.

This climber gets a final safety check from the instructor before going out the window.

A climber descends on rappel, while the belayer controls the descent from below.

A rappelling climber is protected by a standing hip belay.

The brake system of rappelling is recommended for a descent from an overhang.

some disadvantages, it's not used as often as the brake system.

The brake system of rappelling offers more control than the body rappel and is more comfortable. Because the rope isn't wrapped around the body, the problem of rope burns is eliminated. It's a far superior technique when rappelling from an overhang with your full weight on the rope. The major disadvantage of the brake rappel is that it requires additional equipment.

Like the body rappel, the brake system depends on friction for control. However, instead of creating it by wrapping the rope around your body, the rope bends sharply through the climbing hardware, producing enough friction to enable your lower hand to easily control the descent. This type of rappel is done in a seat sling or a swami belt. The brake system is attached to the seat with two or more carabiners. The gates on the carabiners are reversed so they can't possibly open at the same time.

A major problem in brake rappelling is the ever-present danger of getting something pulled into the system. Be sure to keep long hair, beards, clothing, and helmet straps away from the rope. If something should become jammed in the system, stay calm and carefully work it loose. If you need to stop part way down a rappel, wrapping the rope around your leg a few times will hold you in place temporarily. The last person down the rappel should check the rope as he or she descends, to make sure it isn't twisted and that it will not catch in the rock when it's retrieved.

9

Bouldering

Climbers have found that much can be learned by working on difficult rock problems near the ground. For years this type of exercise was considered strictly preparation. Practicing on boulders was part of a conditioning program for big climbs. The military, which used this activity in its training, called it "trick climbing."

In recent years bouldering has becoming a sport in its own right, a specialized form of rock climbing. It takes a great deal of strength and control and is extremely demanding. Yet the benefits are many.

You can improve your skills by working beyond your ability with minimal risk. By repeating a maneuver again and again, you can discover the best way of doing it. Strength and technique on long traverses can be developed without the added distraction of a great amount of exposure.

If you're using bouldering as preparation, take care to develop good habits, because they are sure to carry

Bouldering is far from easy. It is definitely not for those who are allergic to scraped knuckles. Don't be discouraged. Many practice sessions are required to get the hang of the sport. When you have mastered a difficult route, you'll find that the joy of disciplined motion is a highly satisfying, very personal achievement.

Perhaps you will agree with John Gill, who describes bouldering as "the fascinating acrobatic synthesis of man and rock." For him, it is no less than the soul of rock climbing.

10

Rating Climbs

Rating systems have been developed to give climbers a general idea of the difficulty of a route. It is essential to remember that no two climbs are ever alike. Rock slides, weather, and other climbers can drastically affect conditions. Also, climbers' abilities vary from day to day. Their opinions of what is easy and what is hard are influenced by their own experiences. In other words, the rating systems were created by human beings, which means, unfortunately, that they are far from perfect. However, you'll find it's a big help to have some idea of what's ahead.

Two major rating systems are used today in the United States and Canada, but there are a number of regional variations. Most systems are divided into six or seven classifications, with seven being an impossible climb. This might mean an extremely steep cliff of rotten rock that will not hold equipment.

Grade 1. Basically, this is an easy uphill hike, requiring no special equipment. You can walk the entire way with your hands in your pockets if you wish.

Grade 2. You'll need proper shoes or boots because rough hiking conditions may make for tricky footing. Your hands may be needed occasionally for balance, but anyone who can climb a ladder can handle this one with ease.

Grade 3. This is a steeper climb, one that requires the frequent use of your hands. You'll need to think ahead and plan the placement of both feet and hands. Ropes should be available, especially for beginners.

Grade 4. The nature of the rock, complex handholds and footholds, and a good deal of exposure make special equipment necessary. A rope is required. Belays must be used for safety, and pitons may be needed to anchor belays. The leader should be an expert climber.

Grade 5. This is for the pros. Most climbers will use direct aid, and all should have pitons or bolts available for protection in case of a fall.

Grade 6. The absence of natural cracks in the rock means that pitons or bolts must be used for direct-aid climbing.

For a number of years, these ratings gave a general idea of what kind of equipment would be required, but technical climbers soon found that all their routes were rated either 5 or 6. Because there were many differences between climbs that had been given the same grade, a decimal system was added. A 5.0 climb would be far easier, for instance, than a 5.8.

Another helpful addition to rating classifications was provided by the Yosemite system, which added Roman numerals to give an approximate idea of the time required for a climb. Remember that these are estimates only and that they are based on good conditions. Grade I usually takes just a few hours. Grade II will require half a day, and Grade III most of the day. Grade IV may take a long day or one-and-a-half days. Grade V will take from one to two days. Climbers should allow several days to complete Grade VI.

The National Climbing Classification System (NCCS) adds letter symbols to its numbered grades. An *F* stands for free climbing, meaning that equipment is used only for protection, not for making progress up the rock. If aid is needed, it is indicated by the letter *A*. Aid, or direct aid, as it's often called, means hardware is needed to support a climber's weight.

The most complete classifications indicate estimates of the length of time, difficulty, and equipment needs for a climb, but keep in mind that a change in conditions can drastically alter a route. An ice storm may transform a grade 2 climb into a 5 in short order. Also, the grade is given for the most challenging section of the climb. Very few routes are of the same difficulty all the way up. In fact, one climb may have all six grades represented along the route.

Beginners should master each grade before moving on to the next one. Don't be shy about asking other climbers exactly what to expect on different routes. After you've had some experience on the rocks and become familiar with an area's rating system, you'll have a better idea of what lies above.

11

Weather

Do you know how to treat hypothermia? The best way to avoid being hit by lightning? Why a hat is so important when the weather turns cold?

Climbers who don't know the answers to these questions may find themselves in deep trouble. You must be prepared to cope with all kinds of problems because the weather in most mountain ranges changes so quickly. When you start a climb, the sky may be beautifully blue and absolutely cloudless. Yet, twenty minutes later, dark thunderheads could threaten.

The safest way to deal with a storm is to avoid it. You begin before leaving your warm dry house by studying the latest weather forecasts for the area. These can give you a general idea of trends, but you'll also have to become familiar with the weather patterns peculiar to the mountains you'll climb. Some ranges have a reputation for afternoon thunderstorms, others for gusty winds.

Even after becoming familiar with the patterns of a

particular range of mountains, you will find second-guessing the weather an inexact science. Some general information may help. The higher up the mountain you go, the colder it will be. The temperature usually drops approximately 3.3 degrees every thousand feet, because the thinner the air is, the less heat it holds. When the warm air moving across the lowlands meets the mountains, it is forced to rise. The water in it condenses as the air cools and frequently falls in the form of rain, sleet, or snow.

Because mountain weather is tricky, you probably will have to contend with unpleasant conditions every once in a while. If you are prepared and know how to protect yourself, you'll be able to look at weather changes as part of the adventure of climbing. If not, your day could end in tragedy.

By getting an early start, you may be able to avoid afternoon thunderstorms if they are standard in your area. If you're already climbing and see an approaching storm, it pays to know the best route for a quick descent. Lichen-covered rocks are treacherous in the rain. A rope becomes heavy when soaked and puts a strain on both the climbers and their anchors.

Lightning is always potentially dangerous, and you should take all possible precautions to avoid being struck. Some climbers become so absorbed in their progress that they forget to keep a watchful eye for a quick buildup of clouds. Sudden wind gusts may also be a storm warning. You can recognize the buildup of atmospheric electricity in a number of ways. Your scalp may feel prickly and your hair might crackle or stand on end. Exposed skin feels as if it's been touched by a spider's web.

If you're caught in a thunderstorm, stay off peaks and ridges and away from tall trees. Lightning hits the high places, often many times in the same day. When lightning strikes, its charge on the mountain runs along the ground in currents. These currents are strongest near the place the lightning hits, but they can kill people who are some distance away.

Your primary concern should be to keep out of the path of the electricity, which always follows the line of least resistance. It's important not to let your body bridge a gap that might be in the way of the electricity. If the current runs between your hands and feet, it will pass through your heart. Overhangs, chimneys, and caves are no protection against ground currents and should be avoided. Rappelling is highly dangerous because the lightning is likely to follow the rope. The best position is one with knees drawn up and both feet together. Your hands should not touch the rock. Squatting on a pack or rope will help insulate your body from the ground.

Unfortunately, you can have weather-related problems even on a clear day. Rays of the sun are of much greater intensity and burn far more quickly in the higher altitudes than they do in the lowlands. The best defense is to cover up with as much clothing as possible and to apply commercial products that block ultraviolet rays to all exposed skin. Sunglasses will protect your eyes from excessive glare. Wearing a hat or bandana may help you avoid sunstroke. In very hot weather, it's wise to do your really tough climbing early in the morning or late in the afternoon.

In dry weather, you must be careful to avoid becoming dehydrated. Even if the air feels cool, hard work—which brings on heavy breathing and sweating—can rapidly deplete the moisture in your body. Becoming dehydrated is serious anywhere, but it is especially dangerous when climbing. The person suffering from a loss of fluids may begin to lose energy, have a headache, become dizzy, or get muscle cramps. If not corrected, the condition may be fatal. Drink plenty of water before starting out. In extremely hot, dry weather, carry as much as a gallon of water a day per person. Beginning climbers are tempted to skimp on quantity because water is heavy to haul around, but those who skimp may pay a price.

Because mountain weather is so changeable, it doesn't take long for a really hot day to become hand-numbing cold. The climber who is prepared for a variety of weather conditions will usually be in no great danger. Because as much loss as 40 percent of the body's heat can occur in the head, a hat is a necessary part of your gear. Remember that wool clothing, unlike other fabrics, will keep you warm even when it's wet.

Wind will chill you at an astonishing rate. A temperature of 10° F., combined with a 20-mph-wind, will cool you as rapidly as −25° F. without any air stirring. The most obvious danger from this wind-chill factor is frostbite. Anyone familiar with the great mountain climbs of the world knows how often the price of victory was paid in lost fingers and toes. Frostbite is a possibility any time the temperature gets below freezing, particularly if it's windy. Prevention in the form of gloves, extra dry socks, and boots that fit well is recommended. If climbers are adequately dressed, get plenty of food and liquids, and keep moving, they will probably be all right. If conditions are severe, the first areas affected will be the face, fingers, and toes. The skin usually loses feeling before it starts to freeze, so a climber may not be aware of this problem. Watch for skin that looks whiter than usual. If it has started to freeze, get to work immediately warming the affected area. Be careful not to rub it with snow or heat it too close to the fire.

Anyone who is in danger of frostbite is probably already suffering from hypothermia. News reports call it exposure. This chilling of the body's core is by far the most common weather-related cause of mountain accidents. Many deaths supposedly resulted from falling or errors in judgment have actually been caused by hypothermia. When the body loses more heat than it can produce, blood flow is restricted in arms and legs. They then become susceptible to frostbite. If heat continues to be lost, the mind becomes affected.

One of the greatest problems of hypothermia is that a person is often completely unaware of what is happening. He or she may do exactly the wrong thing to treat it because thinking has become irrational. Be alert for symptoms in yourself and your companions. Shivering, an intense feeling of cold, pale skin, bluish lips and nails, staggering or falling, slurred speech, blurred vision, and odd behavior are all signs that should be heeded. The affected climber who doesn't get adequate water and food, who stays in cold wet clothes and continues working even when exhausted, will soon begin to lose reasoning power. If someone else doesn't recognize the problem before this stage, the person may become unconscious and die. The colder the body gets, the longer the recovery will take, so it's essential to stop heat loss as soon as possible.

The climber should be taken out of the wind, put into dry clothes, and given a hot drink. Put the victim in a sleeping bag with someone, and if necessary, give mouth-to-mouth resuscitation. Lower the person's head slightly in order to keep as much blood as possible flowing to the brain. Even if your friend recovers and looks all right, you should get him or her off the mountain. It takes several days to recover from severe hypothermia; during that time, the person is too weak to continue climbing.

Those who plan to be in the mountains only in the summer may think they don't have to worry about the cold, but hypothermia has claimed victims in 45° F. weather. Because it often seems to strike almost without warning in above-freezing temperatures, every climber needs to be alert to its hazards. As with most mountain problems, the way to ward it off is by intelligent preparation.

12

Health
And Safety

Climbers are masters of their own fates. There is no law against climbing without a helmet or rappelling on a 200-pound-test fish line. The secret to staying alive is found in each participant's attitude. In most situations common sense and good judgment will protect you.

Rock climbing is a potentially dangerous activity, but it is possible to cut the risks to an absolute minimum. Your first line of defense against accidents is preparation, which may make the difference between a memorable adventure and death. Climbers who take precautions before they ever set foot on the rock are the ones who not only survive but survive in style.

Preparation isn't something that should be done only on the day before a climb. Staying in good physical condition is an ongoing obligation to yourself. Learn all you can about contending with emergencies by talking with experienced climbers and by reading articles and books on the subject. Anyone venturing far from civili-

zation should have a basic knowledge of first aid. In a crisis you'll have to rely on your own resources.

Have a good idea of your own abilities and those of your companions. One of the most frequent causes of mishaps is choosing a route that is too difficult. Plenty of practice close to the ground or on easy climbs will help you assess your skill level. Before selecting a new route, talk with other climbers and study guidebooks to make sure you don't get in over your head.

Should you have the urge to try a climb that is clearly beyond your ability, ask yourself why. If you feel you have to prove yourself by risking your life, you're in the wrong sport. Choose an activity that won't endanger others. Mountain rescues are time-consuming and costly. A show-off decision to tackle an impossible climb will not be appreciated.

Physical and mental preparation are vital to the success of your expedition, but just as important is the selection of your companions and equipment. Both must be absolutely reliable in situations of utmost stress. Before each outing check your gear to be sure it is in A-1 condition. Try to anticipate the unexpected. If a fall results in a broken leg and a day trip stretches far into the night, having a flashlight in your pack can make all the difference.

Carry enough food and water, and be sure your first-aid kit is well stocked. It should contain a mild antiseptic, aspirin, salt tablets, adhesive tape, bandages and sterile gauze pads, a snake-bite kit, a pair of scissors or a single-edge razor blade, elastic bandages, matches in a water-proof container, safety pins, medicine a doctor has pre-scribed for you, a sunscreen lotion that blocks ultraviolet rays, and insect repellent.

Leave the details of your trip with someone. Include the route you plan to take, the people you're with, and an estimated time of return. The information should contain the name and phone number of someone to notify if you fail to get back within a reasonable time. Perhaps the person should be a climbing friend or the sheriff or rangers stationed nearest the area where you plan to climb.

Spare clothing—including shoes—and extra water and food should be left in your car. As you hike off on a fair day, this may seem an unnecessary precaution, but there may be a time when you would cheerfully sell your soul for a sip of water or a pair of dry shoes.

Know when to turn back from an expedition. If a storm is brewing, if you run into rotten rock, or if you are having an off day for some reason, don't let false pride make a fool of you. Many accidents in the mountains have occurred because climbers ignored any number of obvious warnings, ranging from their own exhaustion to ominous clouds on the horizon.

If you are climbing at high elevations, you might have to retreat because of physical problems caused by the altitude. A sudden dry cough may be a symptom of pulmonary edema, a rare but serious lung problem. The climber should be taken off the mountain as soon as possible and put under a doctor's care.

Altitude sickness is much more common. It is caused by a shortage of oxygen in the rarified air above 10,000 feet. Some climbers' reactions are feelings of extreme tiredness or nausea. The best way to prevent the problem is by getting used to the altitude gradually. Get plenty of rest, eat lightly, dress comfortably, and climb slowly. For those already suffering from the effects of altitude, the primary cure is rest, although some people respond to a motion-sickness drug.

The major cause of accidents is carelessness. Knowing when climbers are most likely to let down their guard may help you to be extra alert at those times. Climbers are especially vulnerable after completing a difficult pitch. Unfortunately, when the tension lets up, so do they.

Because of this, more accidents happen to climbers coming down from a long climb than going up. This may be the result of a combination of factors—fatigue, waning light, and rushing because of deteriorating weather conditions. A significant contributing cause may be that the climber feels relaxed and overconfident. The time to let down is when you are safe at home, not before.

At some point in your climbing career, you're bound to slip and fall. If you are on a gradual slope, whether it is grassy or rocky, try to turn on your stomach with your legs hanging down and use your hands and toes as brakes. On a steeper slope, you'll be wearing a helmet and climbing with a rope. If you and your belayer have practiced rope handling until it is automatic, you'll have no problem. If you're taking chances and climbing un- roped, then you'll have to trust to luck.

Solo climbing is the ultimate risk. Inexperienced climbers don't belong on the rocks alone any more than beginning swimmers belong in a pool by themselves. Few experts are comfortable with the idea of soloing because they have known of deaths that resulted; they may even have lost a good friend in that way. Great solo ascents make fascinating reading. If you'll let your thrills in this department be vicarious, you won't end up as a tragic climbing statistic.

Preventing an accident is easier than dealing with the result. You can significantly reduce the possibility of a mishap by constantly using your brain. Remember, the ultimate responsibility for being on the rock belongs to you.

13

Ethics and Environment

At first glance, rock looks as if it will last forever. Yet it is actually very fragile. Unfortunately, a mountain can neither heal nor renew itself. A flake that has been broken off will not grow back. Holes drilled in a cliff are there forever. Repeated placement and removal of pitons may completely destroy a crack system in a relatively short time.

Because there are only so many surfaces on which to climb, every possible means must be used to preserve them. In the earth's history, the mutilation of its rock is a rather recent problem. As usual, the culprits are humans. In the beginning, so few dared to climb that the idea of anyone defacing a mountain was laughable. But after those first adventurers let the word out about the exhilaration of climbing and the magnificence of the mountains, the sport took off. Some Alpine peaks suffered from a population explosion as parties swarmed toward the summits. They did little permanent damage, however, because

The fragile beauty of the climbing environment must be preserved.

they were not armed with any rock-scarring equipment. The real crisis was brought about by technology. Specialized equipment enabled men to attempt climbs that were increasingly sensational. Hammers, pitons, bolts, and even drills appeared on mountain faces as a new breed of "rock engineers" chopped their way to the top.

Artificial aids have been controversial since they were first introduced. Although some climbers used equipment sparingly and only on cliffs that would otherwise have been impossible, others of mediocre ability began to substitute mechanical protection for climbing skill. The purists in the sport were appalled at finding bolt ladders next to climbable cracks. They referred to their aid-crazed compatriots as "iron mongers" and "mad bolters."

Permanent rock damage, it soon became apparent, was ruining some of the world's classic climbs. Also, the original spirit of the sport was being defiled. Scrambling up a bolt ladder, placed by someone else, eliminated the need for route finding. Relying heavily on equipment took the edge off the challenge and eliminated the sense of adventure that had been one of climbing's greatest attractions.

In the last twenty-five years a new "clean" climbing ethic was evolved. Destroying holds and chipping at the rock to make new ones is considered the worst possible form. In some areas new climbers who arrive on the scene armed with pitons and piton hammers may be all but run out of town. The strict code of ethics that grew in reaction to the hardware era is vital to the sport. In most places climbing is still basically an unregulated activity. If participants want to preserve their environment and at the same time not give up their freedom to outside control, they must police themselves.

The growing trend away from aids and toward free climbing is a triumph of style. In their quest for ultimate challenges, enthusiasts are leaning more on their own physical performances and less on equipment. They are no longer obsessed with reaching the summit at any price. Exemplary style has come to mean taking advantage of natural features of the rock and leaving the route unchanged for others to enjoy. The result has been that standards have been raised to new levels of excellence. Mountains once considered impossible have been scaled. Routes that at one time required direct aid have now been free-climbed. Each generation seems to improve on the performance of the one before.

Climbers have strong feelings about first ascents. Many think of a new route as a work of art that should be preserved as is, especially one that has been climbed in elegant style. Placing additional pitons and bolts in the route to bring the climb down to accommodate persons of lower ability is considered a desecration of the original achievement.

If a route is beyond your skill level, you should try another one or raise your ability before attempting it. Keep in mind that local climbers have definite ideas of what should and what should not be done in their area. It pays to find out what type of equipment is taboo before beginning your ascent. You can take for granted that each route should be left in the same or better condition than you found it.

Plant and animal life in the mountains is highly vulnerable to human invasion because higher elevations typically have such poor soil and short growing seasons. Use wood sparingly, if at all. Everything you take into the mountains should be carried out, even the orange peels.

Climbers have always appreciated the beauty of the mountains and found renewal in the lofty, hard-earned views they enjoyed from the summits. Preservation of the entire rock climbing environment is essential if quality experiences in the uplands are to continue.

14

Where to Climb

Interest in climbing has burgeoned over the past decade. Fortunately, the United States has a wealth of natural resources—from backyard cliffs to exotic mountain ranges.

You can meet others who share your interest by joining a club or taking classes. To find out where you can get instruction, ask your local chamber of commerce, sporting goods store, or science museum if there is a rock climbing or mountaineering group in your area. Sometimes the YMCA or YWCA offers courses, or there may be a climbing school nearby. Some summer camps and private secondary schools have strong programs, and more and more colleges are offering mountaineering courses for credit. They are often listed under sporting goods in the Yellow Pages.

Most climbing and outing clubs are multipurpose in nature. They may be interested in backpacking, hiking, cave exploring, and canoeing, as well as rock climbing

Crossing from one peak to another via a "fixed line" is known as a Tyrolean traverse.

and mountaineering. Those that stress climbing sometimes ask prospective members to demonstrate technical proficiency, but many are family-oriented clubs with very few restrictions regarding membership. Even university and college clubs will often accept members from their geographic area. Clubs are usually looking for interested new members, and most are willing to teach skills to an eager beginner.

The fact that a club produces publications generally indicates that it is well organized and has been in existence for some time. The only way to decide about a particular group is to take a close look. Check to see if they offer training sessions, sponsor expeditions, and lend or rent equipment, and find out if they welcome new members.

Alaska

Mountaineering Club of Alaska
Box 2037
Anchorage, Alaska 99510
(Publications)

Arizona

Arizona Mountaineering Club
4225 South 47th Place
Phoenix, Arizona 85040
(Publications)

Challenge/Discovery
Prescott College
Prescott, Arizona 86301

California

Boot and Blister Club
HSU
Arcata, California 95521

California Alpine Club
244 Pacific Building
San Francisco, California 94103

The Outing Club
San Diego State College
San Diego, California 92115

The Sierra Club*
1050 Mills Tower
220 Bush Street
San Francisco, California 94101
(Publications)

Stanford Alpine Club
Stanford University
Stanford, California 94305

West Valley Hiking Club
c/o Leon Berthiaume
Grant Avenue
Campbell, California 95008

*Chapters in most major cities and regions of United States.

Colorado

Colorado State Mountaineers
Colorado State University
Fort Collins, Colorado 80521

Denver University Alpine Club
2050 East Evans
Denver, Colorado 80210

Colorado Mountain Club
1723 East 16th Avenue
Denver, Colorado 80218
(Publications)

The Outing Club
University of Colorado
Boulder, Colorado 80302

The Outing Club
University of Northern
Colorado
Greeley, Colorado 80631

Connecticut

Yale Mountaineering Club
Yale University
New Haven, Connecticut 06520

District of Columbia

Potomac Appalachian Trail
Club
1718 N Street, N.W.
Washington, D.C. 20036
(Publications)

Hawaii

Hawaiian Trail and Mountain
Club
P.O. Box 2238
Honolulu, Hawaii 96804

Idaho

Idaho Alpine Club
Idaho Falls, Idaho 83401

Illinois

Chicago Mountaineering Club
2801 South Parkway
Chicago, Illinois 61801

Simian Outing Society
Office of Campus Programs
110 Student Services Building
University of Illinois
Champaign, Illinois 61820

Iowa

The Iowa Mountaineers
P.O. Box 163
Iowa City, Iowa 52240

Iowa State University
Mountaineering Club
107 State Gym
Ames, Iowa 50010

Kansas

Great Plains Mountaineering
Wichita State University
Wichita, Kansas 67208

99

Maryland

Mountain Club of Maryland
c/o H. H. Camper Haven
424 North Eutaw Street
Baltimore, Maryland 21201

Massachusetts

Appalachian Mountain Club*
5 Joy Street
Boston, Massachusetts 02108
(Publications)

Harvard University
Mountaineering Club
Harvard University
Cambridge, Massachusetts 02135
(Publications)

Intercollegiate Outing Club
Association
Cutter House
Smith College
Northampton, Massachusetts
01063
(Publications)

MIT Outing Club
Massachusetts Institute of
Technology
Cambridge, Massachusetts 02139
(Publications)

Tufts Mountain Club
P.O. Box 28
Tufts University Branch
Medford, Massachusetts 02153

*Chapters throughout the Northeast.

Minnesota

Minnesota Rovers
P.O. Box 14133
University Station
Minneapolis, Minnesota 55414

Missouri

St. Louis University Grotto
20 North Grand Boulevard
St. Louis, Missouri 63103

Montana

Rocky Mountaineers
2100 South Avenue West
Missoula, Montana 59801

New Hampshire

Dartmouth Outing Club
Robertson Hall
Dartmouth College
Hanover, New Hampshire 03755
(Publications)

New Jersey

Princeton Mountaineering Club
Princeton University
Princeton, New Jersey 08540

New Mexico

New Mexico Mountain Club
P.O. Box 4151
Albuquerque, New Mexico
87106

The Outing Club
University of New Mexico
Albuquerque, New Mexico
87106

New York

Adirondack Mountain Club*
172 Ridge Street
Glens Falls, New York 12801
(Publications)

The American Alpine Club
113 East 90th Street
New York, New York 10028
(Publications, restricted
membership)

Clarkson College Outing Club
Clarkson College of Technology
Potsdam, New York 13676

Ohio

Ohio State Mountaineers
Ohio State University
Columbus, Ohio 43210

Ohio University Alpine Club
Baker Center
Ohio University
Athens, Ohio 45701

University of Cincinnati
Mountaineering Club
Tangeman University Center
Cincinnati, Ohio 45221

*Chapters in most major cities in
the state.

Oregon

Eugene Mountain Rescue
920 Hoover Lane
Eugene, Oregon 97404

Mazamas
909 Northwest 19th Street
Portland, Oregon 97207

Obsidians
Lane YMCA
Eugene, Oregon 97403

Outdoor Programs
Erb Memorial Union, Room 23
University of Oregon
Eugene, Oregon 97403

Pennsylvania

Explorers Club of Pittsburgh
c/o Mountain Trail Shop
5435 Walnut Street
Pittsburgh, Pennsylvania 15232

Penn State Outing Club
Penn State University
University Park, Pennsylvania
16802

Texas

The Outing Club
Texas Tech University
Lubbock, Texas 79409

Utah

Wasatch Mountain Club
c/o Dr. Paul Horton
3155 Highland Drive
Salt Lake City, Utah 84106

Virginia

The Outing Club
University of Virginia
Charlottesville, Virginia 22903

The Outing Club
c/o Bob Smiley
Virginia Polytechnic Institute
Blacksburg, Virginia 24061

Washington

Outing Club
University of Washington
Seattle, Washington 98105

The Mountaineers
719 Pike Street
Seattle, Washington 98101
(Publications)

Washington State University
Alpine Club

Washington State University
Pulmann, Washington 99163

West Virginia

West Virginia University Outing
Club
336 A Stewart Street
Morgantown, West Virginia
26505

Wisconsin

Hoofers Outing Club
University of Wisconsin
800 Langton Street
Madison, Wisconsin 55706

Wyoming

The Outing Club
University of Wyoming
Laramie, Wyoming 82071

Canada

Alpine Club of Canada*
P.O. Box 1026
Banff, Alberta TOL OCO
Canada
(Publications)

East coast climbers migrate to the Appalachians, a range of mountains that extends from New England into the deep South. A favorite climb is Mount Washington in New Hampshire. At 6,288 feet above sea level, it is the highest peak in the northeastern section of the country.

The Adirondack Mountains in upper New York State cover an area larger than Yosemite, Yellowstone, and Glacier National Parks combined. Climbing is unrestricted, and there is literally something for everyone.

*Sections in most major cities.

102

Beginners may scramble on low-angle slabs; experts will have their work cut out for them when they take on vertical exposed rock and overhanging crags.

George Willig learned on New York cliffs. As a young man he haunted the Schawangunks near New Paltz, about one hundred miles north of New York City. This seven-mile escarpment, with nearly vertical 200-foot faces, proved to be an excellent training ground. Willig received nation-wide publicity when he tested his skills by scaling the New York World Trade Center building. Later, millions witnessed his breath-stopping climb in Utah on the "Wide World of Sports" television program.

Climbing is a relatively new passion for southerners. What they lack in lengthy history, they are making up in current enthusiasm. In 1976 about 300 climbers were belaying each other at Stone Mountain State Park in North Carolina. By 1978 the number had soared to 4,251. Located near the Blue Ridge Parkway, Stone Mountain has gained a reputation as a superb spot for climbers of all levels of experience. Seasoned enthusiasts claim it is the best rock climbing area in the South. The mountain, estimated to be 300 million years old, crests in a spectacular 600-foot dome. When the weather is halfway decent, all thirteen ascent routes on the south face echo with calls of "On belay!"

Most climbing areas in this country have no restrictions. However, if you plan to explore cliffs on private property, be sure to get the owner's permission first.

Some of the best climbing in the western part of the country is found in our national parks. Several major parks and national monuments regulate climbing activities, and most offer instruction. Perhaps you could combine an opportunity to increase your skills with a family vacation. Because of the boom in climbing interest, you should be sure to write for information and reservations well in advance of a visit to a park.

Devils Tower, an 865-foot column of rock in Wyoming, was once used as a landmark by covered wagon caravans pushing their way west. Geologists say the symmetrical tower is the remains of a molten formation from early volcanic activity. Besides being the most conspicuous rock formation in northeastern Wyoming, it is the tallest of its kind in the United States. Devils Tower's nearly perpendicular sides have always attracted climbers. Park rangers offer introductory classes at this splendid scenic attraction, which became the country's first national monument in 1906. Experts must register at monument headquarters and receive approval of the superintendent before attempting an ascent. They are required to show they are physically capable, have the proper equipment, and have had experience in similar hazardous climbing. (For information write to Superintendent, Devils Tower National Monument, Devils Tower, Wyoming 82714.)

While you're in Wyoming, don't miss the Grand Tetons just south of Yellowstone Park. This forty-mile-long cluster of jagged, snow-capped peaks has long been a center for Alpine-style mountaineering. Grant Teton, at 13,770 feet, is considered a major North American climbing peak. At Jenny Lake the Exum School of Mountaineering holds classes for every level of ability, from elementary to advanced. The Grand Teton Climber's Ranch is operated by the American Alpine Club as a dorm and cooking area for registered mountaineers. Because the terrain is so rugged, solo climbing is not advised. (For information write to Superintendent, Grand Teton National Park, Moose, Wyoming.)

Rocky Mountain National Park in western Colorado draws climbers from all over the country. If you'd like to hike to the summit of Longs Peak—at 14,255 feet, the park's highest—check first at the nearest ranger station. For those who prefer rock climbing to hiking, lessons are given by the Rocky Mountain Guide Service and Mountaineering School, which is an approved park concession. You must get permission from the superintendent before climbing the popular "Diamond."

Rangers advise novices to stay on routes that are well within their ability and to turn back if the weather threatens. Those unfamiliar with conditions in the Rockies are amazed at how quickly these mountains can brew up a severe storm. Solo climbing is prohibited. (For information write to Superintendent, Rocky Mountain National Park, Estes Park, Colorado 80517.)

Zion National Park in Utah is a pristine wilderness of high plateaus, deep canyons, and broad mesas. Massive rock formations—among the most brilliantly colored in the world—provide dramatic scenery as well as challenging climbing. The central feature of the park is Zion Canyon, a deep, vertically-walled chasm. If you're looking for a steep trail, the climb up and down Lady Mountain is only two miles, but it takes about five hours. Before scaling these red sandstone walls, climbers must get permission from the superintendent at park headquarters. (Write to Superintendent, Zion National Park, Springdale, Utah 84767.)

California's Yosemite National Park in the Sierra Nevadas has a well-deserved reputation as the center of rock climbing in this country. The setting is grand, and the climate is conducive to nearly year-round activity. A semipermanent rock climbing community has raised standards of the sport to awesome heights. The valley, seven miles long and one mile wide, is bounded by granite walls, domes, and peaks rising 2,000 to 4,000 feet. Overlooking the tranquil scene is El Capitan, a massive monolith that for years was ignored by climbers because of its towering height. If you want to follow in the great traditions of Yosemite climbers and take lessons in this incredibly beautiful "classroom," there is a climbing school as well as a guide service in the area. To protect those who wish to scale the sheer granite faces, park officials ask that you register at the visitor center and report in immediately on returning from your climb. (For information write to Superintendent, Yosemite National Park, California 95389.)

The concession guide service at Mount Rainier National Park in the state of Washington conducts a varied program for both novices and experienced climbers. Rainier is 14,410 feet, the highest peak in the state, as well as in the whole Cascade Range. The Americans who scaled Mount Everest in 1963 used Mount Rainier as their training ground. The climb to the summit is a long, strenuous ascent over moderately difficult terrain. If you are in good condition and go with a group, previous experience is not necessary to successfully reach the top. An expert guide, who can spot treacherous crevasses and crumbling lava, is a necessity. The climb takes two days. The first night is spent at Camp Muir, a rock shelter at 10,000 feet. Shortly after midnight, climbers rope up for the final push. The reason for the early departure is to give the group a chance to reach the top and get back before the sun brings danger from icefall. Routes are officially open from May 30 to Labor Day. All climbers must register and give evidence that they are properly qualified and equipped. (For information write to Superintendent, Mount Rainier National Park, Longmire, Washington 98397.)

If nothing less than the highest point on the continent is your goal, then it's off to Alaska's Mount McKinley. No wonder it was called *Denali,* the Indian word for "The Big One"; the peak is 20,320 feet high. McKinley straddles the center of the Alaskan Range, the northernmost extension of the Rocky Mountains. Climbing expeditions must be ready to contend with the most severe winter conditions even in mid-summer. Wind-chill factors of $-148°$ F. have been recorded. Besides battling extreme cold and altitude sickness, climbers struggle against avalanches, crevasses, blowing snow, and winds of 60 to 70 mph. The scenic West Buttress route, the one most frequently used, follows one of Alaska's longest glaciers. Since the first successful assault of the mountain's south peak in 1913, more than 3,500 climbers have attempted the ascent. About 2,000 have been successful. More than 35 have lost their lives on the mountain. Guide Companies which set up climbing parties must be notified well in advance of the climb. (For information write to Superintendent, Mount McKinley National Park, McKinley Park, Alaska 99755.)

Experts who have had a great deal of experience on mountains in this country sometimes yearn to test themselves in foreign lands. In western Canada three major mountain ranges contain many fine glaciated peaks. Some of the most impressive ones are in Banff and Jasper national parks.

Mexico has its own looming challenges. The country's highest point is a volcanic cone near Mexico City, which is 18,700 feet above sea level. The rugged mountains of the Baja Peninsula are another lure for the adventurous.

You may want to return to the birthplace of mountain climbing. Those who cross the Atlantic to experience the legendary Alps will find differences in accommodations as well as in climbing style. The sport has long been a highly respected activity in Europe, and as a result, Alpine clubs and government agencies maintain a wide network of huts for climbers. Conveniently located for virtually every major route, these refuges range from tiny emergency shelters to large hotels. Sometimes they are reached after a fairly long hike, but once there, you'll find them surprisingly comfortable. You can take all or part of your food, cook it yourself, or have it cooked for you. Someone will wake you at three o'clock on the morning of your ascent. If you are alone and/or inexperienced, guides, available at climbing centers, will make all the arrangements for you. Remember, climbing is such a popular pastime in the Alps that routes up well-known peaks are often crowded, particularly in July and August, the best climbing months.

Other famed climbing areas around the globe include the Andes Mountains in South America and the Himalaya Mountains and the Karakoram Range in Asia. The peaks are so far from roads that expedition members must take several weeks' worth of supplies with them.

Some experts view the ultimate climbing challenges as the peaks of the Arctic regions of Norway, Canada, and Alaska, as well as those in Patagonia at the tip of South America. At these ends of the earth, diabolical weather and a horrendously rugged landscape challenge the most courageous.

Glossary
Of Climbing Terms

Abseil   European term for rappel, controlled sliding descent on a rope

Aid Climbing   climbing that uses equipment for assistance rather than just for protection; opposite of free climbing

Anchor   a place or device to which a climber can attach a rope, particularly the attachment used to secure the belayer to the mountain

Ascent   the climb up

Belay   a system that uses a rope to protect the climber from falling

Belayer   person handling the rope that protects the climber

Bivouac   overnight stay on rock or in mountains, often with minimal equipment

Body rappel   a controlled sliding descent using a rope wrapped around the body in a prescribed way

Bolts   metal devices hammered into holes drilled in the rock

Bouldering sport of climbing, which demands extremely difficult moves and is done close to the ground

Bowline a type of nonslip knot

Brake bar device through which rope is threaded so as to create friction for a controlled rappel

Bucket relatively large handhold or foothold with raised edge

Carabiner oval metal ring with spring loaded gate, used to attach a rope to something while still allowing it to slide freely

Chickenhead rock projection

Chimney a crack wide enough for a climber to fit inside

Chock, chockstone a rock jammed in a crack or chimney

Crux most difficult section of a climb

Descent the route down

Direct aid use of equipment for physical assistance in climbing; also called artificial climbing

Dulfersitz body rappel

Exposure empty space beneath climber, or being subjected to dangerous weather conditions

Face steep wall of rock

Fissure crack

Free climbing climbing in which equipment is used to protect the climber in the event of a fall, but not for moving upward

Friction climbing using the sole of the shoe and palm of the hand against rock for friction, rather than balancing, on ledges or holds

Guide hand the hand that pulls in or lets out the rope on a belay; opposite of brake hand

Gully a crack large enough to walk in

Hand traverse using the hands to climb horizontally

Horn a projection of rock

Hypothermia chilling of the body's core

Jamming a technique in which a part or all of the climber's body is wedged in a crack

Kernmantel rope construction with an inner core of filaments protected by an outer sheath

Klettershoes flexible shoes designed for rock climbing

Layback strenuous technique in which the hands pull while the feet push against the rock for friction

Ledge a narrow shelf

Lichen small plants that grow on the surfaces of rocks

Lieback same as layback

Mantel a technique a climber uses to press himself up onto a shelf

Nut small artificial chockstone, with a wire or sling that is inserted in a crack for protection or support

Open book two vertical cliffs meeting at right angles like walls in the corner of a room

Perlon European trade name for nylon

Pinnacle narrow, free-standing peak of rock

Pitch distance between each stop on a climb

Piton a tapered metal spike that can be hammered into a crack and is used for protection or support

Prusik knot a type of knot that grips the rope tightly when under tension but can be moved upward when the weight is lifted

Rappel Controlled sliding descent on a rope; also called abseil

Roof horizontal overhang

Route course taken on a climb

Scrambling climbing without using a rope

Scree slope of fragmented rock

Slab flat rock

Sling a loop of rope or webbing

Smearing a technique in which the sole of the shoe is squashed into a hold to obtain maximum friction

Spur a projecting ridge

Static belay a belay from above

Swami belt a length of nylon webbing wrapped around the climber's waist

111

Swiss seat seat sling of nylon webbing wrapped around the waist and legs

Talus broken rocks at base of cliff

Technical climbing using equipment for protection or direct assistance

Traverse horizontal route across a cliff or face

Verglas thin film of ice

Wall extremely steep cliff

Index

MIT Outing Club, 100
Manteling, 35, 38
Mazamas, 101
Minnesota Rovers, 100
Mont Blanc, 8
Mount Everest, 8, 9, 106
Mount McKinley, 16, 18, 106–7
Mount Rainier National Park, 106
Mount Washington, 102
Mount Whitney, 102
Mountaineering, 5
Mountaineering Club of Alaska, 98

National Climbing Classification System, 80
New Mexico Mountain Club, 100
Norgay, Tenzing, 9

Obsidians, 101
Ohio State Mountaineers, 101
Ohio University Alpine Club, 101
Outdoor Programs, 101
Outing Clubs
San Diego, 98
Texas Tech University, 101
University of Colorado, 99
University of New Mexico, 101

University of North Colorado, 99
University of Virginia, 102
University of Washington, 102
University of Wyoming, 102
Virginia Polytechnic Institute, 102
West Virginia, 102

Paccard, Michel, 8
Perlon, 111
Pike, Zebulon, 10
Pike's Peak, 11
Pitons, 16, 58, 94, 111
Potomac Appalachian Trail Club, 99
Princeton Mountaineering Club, 100

Rapelling, 58, 60, 67, 73, 84–5, 87, 109
Rating systems, 78–81
Rock damage, 94
Rocky Mountain Guide Service and Mountaineering School, 104–5
Rocky Mountaineers, 100
Rocky Mountains, 12
Romsdalshorn, 8
Ropes, 16, 23–5, 27, 47, 57, 60, 67, 83, 111

Safety systems, 4, 16, 87, 89, 90–1

de Saussure, Horace Benedict, 8
Shawnagunk cliffs, 13, 103
Sierra Club, 98
Simian Outing Society, 99
Slab climbing, 31, 33
Solo climbing, 91
Stone Mountain State Park, 103

Technical climbing, 11, 33
Tufts Mountain Club, 100

University of Cincinnati Mountaineering Club, 101

Wasatch Mountain Club, 102

Washington State University Alpine Club, 102
Weather, 78, 80, 82–6, 106
Webbing, 27, 60
West Valley Hiking Club, 98
Willig, George, 102

Yale Mountaineering Club, 99
Yellowstone National Park, 102, 104
Yosemite National Park, 102, 105
Yosemite Valley, 5, 16, 17

Zion National Park, 105

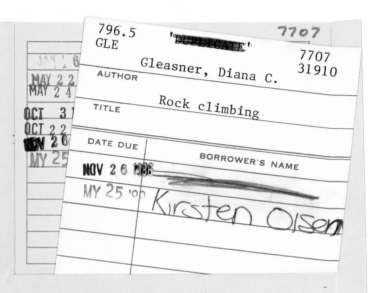

796.5
GLE

Gleasner, Diana C.

Rock climbing.

BRUNSWICK HIGH SCHOOL
MEDIA CENTER